DIFFERENT EYES

living distinctively in a time of uncertainty

GW00705960

Equipping the Church for action

Spring Harvest 2010

Also available in Braille and Giant Print

Published and distributed by
Elevation
14 Horsted Square
Uckfield
East Sussex TN22 1QG

First edition 2010

ISBN   978-1-899788-69-9

SPRING HARVEST 2010
DIFFERENT EYES

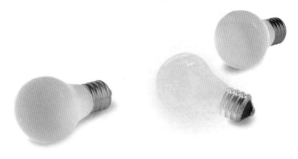

LEARNING
GUIDE

Pete Broadbent, Jeff Lucas,
Russell Rook, Ruth Valerio and
Krish Kandiah (editor)

Spring
Harvest
Equipping the Church for action

Miracles can be tough to live with.

A thirty-year-old man, blind since birth, had an operation that gave him new eyes and normal vision. The never-blind cannot imagine the impact this had on him.

Initially he was euphoric. He could see, for the first time ever.

Then the excitement faded. He became disorientated and depressed. The cause of his descent was a collision with reality. The world he could now see bore little resemblance to the world he had seen in his imagination during thirty years of darkness. He was suffering a deep grief and confusion.

Looking at the world through his new eyes he saw a reality that often contradicted his assumptions. Sight required him to relinquish his fondly held, but often extraordinarily misguided, ideas about what things actually looked like. Not seeking to return to the past, he began praying very hard for another even greater miracle; that God would show him how to live in this strange world.

Our prayer is that at *Spring Harvest 2010 Different Eyes* we will together enjoy the miracle of new and clearer sight. Through God's revelation, we want to see the world differently; with his eyes. To see from a God's eye view. As we struggle to make sense out of what is happening in our world, in our communities, workplaces, homes and churches, we pray that new clarity and vision will bring new possibilities and opportunities.

Spring Harvest's goal is for the *Learning Guide*, which is intended for use in conjunction with the book *Different Eyes* by Steve Chalke and Alan Mann, to help us live with the consequences of all God has done for us and all that he has for us.

Seeing the world with different eyes will cause both celebration and discomfort; pain as well as joy. However, like the man in the story, each of us has to choose whether, in the end, we are happier living with our beloved but possibly misguided notions or focussing on reality.

The theme for *Spring Harvest 2010* can be summed up in a word – ethics.

Unfortunately, most people regard ethics as thinking about difficult and ambiguous moral quandaries: "Should I lie to protect a friend?" "Must we always tell a dying person they are dying?" "Do we have to tell the whole truth all the time, however brutal?" "Can I ever compromise my values to achieve a good goal?"

In fact, ethics are bigger and broader than these questions. Our ethics provide a cultural framework – an under-pinning value system – in which we live our whole lives. Ethics are like the air we breathe; although for the most part they go unnoticed, our lives and communities depend on them. Whether we like it or not, we're all doing ethics all the time with questions such as: "Was it right to grass someone up over the murder of Archie Mitchell?" "Is it right to be so explicit about cancer sufferers in Corrie?" The internet is full of sites where people debate soap opera storylines – and we do the same in real life.

But Christian ethics are distinctive ethics. They are not just anyone's ethics. They are 'uncommon' rather than 'common' sense. Indeed, if Christian ethics are not distinctive, then Jesus is relegated to nothing more than a 'personal' and 'private' motivator, encouraging us to ideals that are shared by all. We do not follow a set of universal moral or ethical principals; we follow Jesus. And in following Jesus we live distinctively, and therefore beautifully.

Christian ethics is a vast subject – and Christians have taken a number of different approaches to the way they tackle day-to-day dilemmas.

Natural law ethics held sway for a long time in Christian history. The idea, based particularly in Catholic theology, is that natural law and divine law are continuous – any rational person will reach the right moral conclusion because we live in an ordered universe that reflects the nature of God. That worked very well while there was a consensus in society.

Rule based approaches have long influenced and shaped Protestant Christianity. Many village churches display the Ten Commandments next to the communion table – and many of us grew up with a Christianity that sought absolute rules to live by. Scripture unavoidably points us towards the law and the perfection standards of a holy God. But how do we then live?

Consequentialist methods of doing ethics emerged in reaction to that kind of approach. Perhaps the most influential Christian book on the subject is Joseph Fletcher's *Situation Ethics*, which argues that the only abiding law is the law of love. Love should determine your moral decisions in every situation. (Joseph Fletcher, *Situation Ethics* (SCM Press, 1966))

The *Learning Guide* explores some of these approaches, but the focus is **virtue ethics**. The first question here isn't "How should we act?" but "What sort of people should we be? How should we live?" There are no foolproof answers to the problems of ethical decision making, and the *Different Eyes Learning Guide* won't try to provide them.

We simply seek to ask: "What tools do we need for the complex moral choices that confront us as we live for Christ in the 21st century? How do we live distinctively in- a time of uncertainty? How do we see the world through different eyes – the eyes of Christ?"

CONTENTS

The God We Worship

Aim

To explore and discover the character of Yahweh.

Learning Objectives

To understand that the way we see God controls the way we see life.

To explore ways in which we can know God better.

Overview

In this session we'll see that:

- The God of Israel is unlike any other deity; he calls himself Yahweh (I am).

- We tend to impose our understandings onto God, imbuing him with our own values, standards, hopes, and attitudes.

- We can't easily define Yahweh; his self-definition is 'I am'. To know God we must journey with him and join his people.

- This journey began at creation. We start to understand God's values, standards, hopes and attitudes through the Old Testament, especially Exodus.

- The Exodus story allows Israel to understand that her history, identity and destiny are wrapped up in God's story.

- God gave his people the Ten Commandments as part of his relationship with them. Their vision of God grew as they became familiar with his holy and just character. The commandments are not an isolated list of prohibitions.

- Holiness is joining the growing moral vision between God and humanity. This can only be done in the context of a loving relationship with God, by joining God's story.

Russell Rook

SESSION 1

Why (theory)

We often assume that the first step in theology is to convince people that God exists. However, the Old Testament, and indeed the entire Bible, is concerned with a different and more important question: What kind of God exists?

For many people, ethics is something they do. But today we won't start with what we do, or don't do, for the simple reason that Christian ethics is primarily about who we know. Our lives as God's people are directed by the God we worship.

Knowing God is enough to transform all that we see and do.

Hundreds of art lovers crammed a gallery, anxious for a first glimpse of the romantic landscape painter's latest works. A rather well-to-do lady turned to her companion and in a voice for all to hear declared, "I've never seen colours like that at sunset!"

Beside her and unknown to the self-styled critic stood the artist. With customary eloquence and tantalising grace he whispered, "But don't you wish you could?"

Because we know the divine artist we can see the world in high-definition full colour. Reality should be more glorious for worshippers. We should see the colours and shades, textures and features that elude others.

We claim to know, worship and enjoy the maker of the heavens and the earth. Everything we see, say and do is transformed with this confession. Our actions are driven by divine revelation.

Who is this God and how can we know him?

Maybe you have heard this joke:

Looking over the shoulder of a budding young artist, the primary school teacher enquired as to what he was working on.

"I'm drawing God," came the reply.

The teacher could hardly hide her surprise.

"But no one knows what God looks like," she said.

"They soon will," the student declared.

Not having seen the drawing, I still don't know what God looks like. We do, however, have the testimony of some eyewitnesses. The angels who surround God's throne use one word to describe him, according to Isaiah and John. Over and over they repeat: "Holy, holy, holy is the Lord" (Isa 6:3, Rev 4:8).

1. What's in a name?

Holiness is the word most often used in the Bible to describe and distinguish God. In singing and speaking of his holiness, we declare that God is unique, unlike anyone or anything in heaven or on earth.

One of the most significant prayers in the Jewish faith is the *Shema*: "Hear, O Israel: the LORD [Yahweh] our God, the LORD is one." (Deut 6:4–9)

Though the Shema is a simple text, it contains a depth of theology. Its chief task is to affirm monotheism. There is only one God, Yahweh, the God of the whole earth, without equal or rival.

This claim remains controversial. Yahweh has never been universally acknowledged as the one true God. Throughout history there have been competing claims for the attention and dedication of his people.

Yahweh may be wholly different from the other gods, but the word 'god' is itself very common. In the Old Testament, the Hebrew '*El*' is a generic word for any 'god'. It doesn't tell us anything about the character of the deity. When the God of Israel reveals himself, he announces that he is more than just another '*El*'.

Addressed by a burning bush, Moses somewhat understandably asks who is talking. The immediate response is 'Yahweh', traditionally translated as 'I am who I am'.

PAUSE FOR THOUGHT

Imagine you're playing a game of word association. What comes to mind when you think about the word 'holy'? What words would others offer in response to 'holy'? What words might those outside of the church add alongside 'holy'?

Generations since have worshipped the great I Am, Yahweh, the God who is true; the one who will be who he is and who he has always been; the God who is different from all the rest. Although 'god' may be a common name, Yahweh isn't. The God of Israel distinguishes himself from 'gods'. He is different, set-apart and, in the words of the heavenly host, holy.

2. What's so special about Yahweh?

The size and scope of God's character and goodness mean we frequently run out of words to describe him. We often talk of his mercy, kindness, faithfulness, sovereignty and providence. Sometimes we talk of his anger, wrath, jealousy, punishment and judgement. And yet the Bible needs only two words to sum up every aspect of God's being. God is 'love' and he is 'holy'.

God's holiness and love are interdependent. God is holy because he is love, and God is love because he is holy. They can be neither separated nor contradicted. Every other aspect of God's character and every divine action, whether comfortable or uncomfortable, is an expression of his love and holiness.

> "Holiness is the pure simplicity of God's love… [and] the dynamic simplicity of the God who is love." (David Willis, *Notes on the Holiness of God* (Eerdmans, 2002))

3. Who not to worship

Other nations derided Israel's monotheism as quaint and foolish. After all, why settle for just one god when you can have many? If you're going to believe in '*El*', the concept of god, why not shorten the odds and worship several?

In the ancient world, worshipping many gods was akin to taking out many insurance policies. One god to ensure the success of local crops, another god to ensure love and fertility, and a third to help in battle.

Despite God's self-revelation to Moses and their forefathers, God's people all too easily slipped into idolatry and infidelity. And yet God persisted, faithfully revealing himself to succeeding generations regardless of his people's faithlessness.

> "Yahweh is insistent: 'Don't confuse me with any other god. And don't try to box me in. ... I am different,'" (Steve Chalke and Alan Mann, *Different Eyes: the art of living beautifully* (Zondervan 2010))

The difference between Yahweh and all the other gods is this; he exists and they don't. He is eternal. They don't exist. He is ever faithful, ever merciful, ever loving and ever kind, but they don't exist. He is like nothing we have ever seen or imagined – and they don't exist.

When we say that God is holy we declare that he is not just one god among many, not just another insurance policy. We declare that the holy God is the one true God.

A government official was once keen to test my ability to serve a multicultural community. He told me about his frustration with the reticence of religious groups to work together and share resources. I listened carefully as he outlined his plan to create a large community centre where all faiths could worship. "After all," he concluded, "you all worship the same god anyway, don't you?"

I told him how I shared his desire to see groups coming together to serve their communities and his frustration at how much mistrust existed between groups, but I could not accept his view that we all worship the same God. The whole of biblical Christianity rests on the reality that God has revealed himself as different, set apart and holy, and his people are called to be different, set apart and holy.

While God knows other gods don't exist and thus are powerless, he also knows the power of the imagination that he gave us. He knows how easily we make gods in our image and worship them with our lives. When we do this we put our faith in an idol, something we think has divine power but is actually our own creation. We may not worship other gods in the hope of a bountiful harvest or in our search for love,

What false gods are we in danger of making or worshipping? What would it take for us to walk away from these and instead worship the one true God?

but we often take out insurance in case God doesn't come through for us.

4. God's holiness and us

"Who this Yahweh is will only be discovered in an ongoing, committed relationship with him." (Chalke and Mann, *Different Eyes*)

Returning to the game of word association, how many of us threw in words such as 'otherness', 'transcendent' or 'set apart'? While undoubtedly correct, if we're not careful these words can lead us down the wrong path.

A mistaken view of holiness can lead us to believe that God is removed from us. We can confuse *difference* with *distance*. And then we can end up identifying people as holy simply because their lives seem removed from the messiness of everyday life.

"Holiness has frequently been claimed by, and associated with, perfectionists who lacked humanity, worriers who were obsessed with their imperfections, or pretenders who could not laugh at themselves. Legalists and lovers of rules have taken the call to holiness and made it into a very unattractive employer. Many people, Christians and non-Christians alike, have become so repulsed by those who very self-consciously strive after moral superiority that they often apply to them the phrase 'holier than thou' to expose the real motivation: one-upmanship." (Phil Needham, *He Who Laughed First: Delighting in a Holy God* (Beacon Hill Press, 2000))

God is beyond us, or transcendent. But the central theme and purpose of the Bible is to reveal that God is not removed from the mess of our world; he is with us, or immanent. Rather than stand by as his people perish, God has chosen to get involved and save them. He is certainly different, but he is certainly not distant.

We must avoid the trap of separating God's transcendence from his immanence. It's clear from the encounter between

Yahweh and Moses, the prince turned criminal turned refugee, that God is both beyond us and present with us.

> "God is closer to me than I am to myself."
> (Jurgen Moltmann and Margaret Kohl, *The Spirit of Life: A Universal Affirmation* (SCM Press, 1992))

God's proximity is an essential aspect of his holiness. It singles him out from the gods and vindicates him as the one true God. As Moses discovered, Yahweh doesn't situate himself in the outer heavens, distancing himself from his creation. Yahweh is not a clock-maker god who has built a machine and is standing back while it runs its course. Yahweh is the God who shows up! He shows up in a burning bush, a miraculous escape, a nation's history, a carpenter's son, a community called church and in you and me, to name just a few.

5. Be holy

The first five books of the Old Testament tell the story of a God who is both immanent and transcendent, and who created to relate. God is a divine relationship; Father, Son and Holy Spirit. His creation and everything he does in his creation is an invitation to relate to him. Creation is God's invitation for us to join in fellowship with the Trinity.

Before creation there was no time, space, energy or substance of any kind. God's originating act was an exercise of God's will and pleasure, an act of love.

In the burning bush, God revealed himself so Moses and his people might follow him out of Egypt, worship him through the wilderness and enter the promised land. Yahweh's meeting with Moses set the stage for a drama.

The months and years after saw a miraculous escape from an oppressive tyrant, a forty-year adventure in the wilderness, the revelation of the Ten Commandments, the crossing of the Jordan River, and the conquest of the Promised Land. When he gives Moses the Ten Commandments, Yahweh tells a story: I am the God who "brought you out of Egypt, out of the land of slavery" (Exod 20:2). Knowing, understanding and living in that story is key to what follows.

However, the Exodus story isn't just the story of a nation. It's the real-life relationship of a people with their God. Through the Exodus experience all the Hebrew people, old and young, male and female, discover that God is involved in their story, and they are entrusted with God's holiness.

That's why retelling the story is central to Jewish worship to this day. It's not simply a stroll down memory lane. Retelling the story is to rediscover the holy God of Israel, the one true God, maker of heaven and earth. It reminds us that God can be experienced in all his holiness whether we are enslaved or free, wandering or settled, lost or found. When we retell the story in our own time and space we claim it as our story, and take our place in God's eternal story. The practice of retelling extends to the Old Testament with *Simchat Torah* (rejoicing with the Torah), which marks the conclusion of the annual cycle of public Torah readings, and the beginning of a new cycle. These festivities begin in the evening with Torah readings and seven circuits of singing and dancing, parading the Torah scrolls around the synagogue.

At the summit, God's holiness shows up in Jesus. Pure holiness joined with pure humanity proves, once and for all, that the holy God is for us and with us.

When we truly know God, God's holiness will be truly reflected in us; in our church, our story, our worship, our mission and our community. The plan of creation, and the purpose of revelation, is to bring glory and worship to God and to be holy as God is holy.

What

1. **Knowing God**

The name Yahweh is an invitation to discover and an enticement to an adventure of slow revelation.

Christian ethics is primarily about the God we know and how our relationship with him should drive all we do. But

PAUSE FOR THOUGHT

Reflect on a time when you unmistakeably saw God's presence in your own story.

How did this occur and what did you learn about God from it?

how do we know God? And how can we be sure that what we know is correct? If our understanding of God is skewed, incorrect or incomplete then our ethics will be similarly wrong. Can fallen and fallible people such as us ever really know God?

The story is told of an enthusiastic young preacher in Scotland whose sermon offended almost every member of the congregation. As the congregation traipsed out onto the damp streets after the service, he stood deflated by the door to shake their hands. Finally an elderly man grabbed him and growled, "Och well, if God can speak through Balaam's ass, I guess he can speak through you!"

When theologians talk about our capacity to know and understand God they often use the word 'mediation'. When they say our knowledge of God is 'mediated', theologians are pointing to the many things that God uses to reveal himself.

God's holiness is so pure it's dangerous. Even Moses never saw God's face. He was only allowed to stand near, facing the other direction, as God passed. Even that little exposure made Moses shine with God's holiness. God also allows us to take part in revealing him to the world, meaning that Christians mediate God's holiness.

But Christians are not the only ones privileged to mediate God. John Calvin wrote: "Creation is the theatre of God's glory." God uses creation, the Bible, the story of Israel, the person of Jesus, the community of the church, and other things besides to mediate. He can even use tactless young preachers. (John Calvin, *Institutes of the Christian Religion*, ed. John T. McNeill, trans. and indexed by Ford Lewis Battles (The Westminster Press, 1967), 1.6.2 (72))

The holiness tradition that dates back to John and Charles Wesley provides one way of thinking about how we know God. Called the Wesleyan Quadrilateral, it uses four different sources to reach theological conclusions. They are:

1. **The Bible**. God reveals himself to us by his word. Supremely authoritative, the Bible provides us with an inspired view of God and human history through the story of creation, Israel, Jesus and the church.

2. **The Church**. The church is critical to understanding who God is. It is entrusted to show and tell the Bible story. In the church, we know and become part of the body of Christ.

3. **Human Reason**. Reason is essential to making sense of God. As we think about God and reflect on his revelation in the Bible and the church we come to know God better.

4. **Human Experience**. Our maker knows us and shows himself in ways and words, situations and sightings that connect with our personal experience.

To know God more fully we should develop all four sources: understanding the Bible, being part of the church, thinking clearly, and experiencing God.

2. Infinitely more

There are modes of knowing God that are particular to each of us. They are affected by our background, personality type, learning style, education, and church experience.

Regardless of our learning style, learning who we are as humans is about understanding how the story of our life fits within a bigger story. That's why certain of the Gospels begin the story of the incarnation with an extended genealogy. We understand Jesus' story by seeing where it fits into the story of his family and nation.

By attaching themselves to God's story and purpose, the children of Israel filled their lives with a deeper purpose and direction. They were part of the great adventure of discovering what God was doing and joining it.

God tells Moses he is Yahweh (I am who I am), sometimes translated as 'I am who I will be'. The first implication of this statement is that he will always be faithful; true to himself as the God who is love and holiness. The second is that it will take God's people a very long time to really know who God is.

PAUSE FOR THOUGHT

Think about each of these four ways in which God makes himself known. How has God used the Bible, church, human reason and experience to make himself known to you?

When God gave the Ten Commandments, the context was his own holy character. How does God intend us to see him according to Exodus 34:4–7?

So Moses chiseled out two stone tablets like the first ones and went up Mount Sinai early in the morning, as the LORD had commanded him; and he carried the two stone tablets in his hands. Then the LORD came down in the cloud and stood there with him and proclaimed his name, the LORD. And he passed in front of Moses, proclaiming, "The LORD, the LORD, the compassionate and gracious God, slow to anger, abounding in love and faithfulness, maintaining love to thousands, and forgiving wickedness, rebellion and sin. Yet he does not leave the guilty unpunished; he punishes the children and their children for the sin of the fathers to the third and fourth generation."

Christians too easily default to a fixed view of God as more 'I am who I was' than 'I am who I will be', and yet the God of the Bible is gloriously open ended. This doesn't mean that God is inconsistent or that he changes. God has shown us everything we need to know about him, although there is infinitely more to him than we have yet seen or imagined.

God shields us, as he shielded Moses on the mountain, from his holiness, showing us only the bits that are right for us.

The eternal scope of God's holiness means that he can always surprise us. The eternal scope of his love will always transform us. As we get to know God better, we see new dimensions of his character, join the great adventure of his perfect plan and prepare to see him face to face.

How

Choose one of the following scenarios and use either the Wesleyan Quadrilateral or the Bible passage above to help.

1. Church

Your church has discovered that an active member was disciplined for misconduct while an elder in a previous church. How should the leadership respond? How does knowing the multifaceted splendor of God's character as revealed in Exodus 34 help you to know what to do?

2. Relational

"Why is God so miserable? Why has he got such a downer on everything we do? Don't do this and don't do that. Don't desire what other people have got. Don't lie. Don't commit adultery. It's pathetic." (Bill Armstrong, May 2009, http://www.baycma. org/index_files/Page2009.htm quoted in *Different Eyes*)

Draft a response to this using the Wesleyan Quadrilateral – what we know about God from our primary authority the Bible and also through the church, reason and experience.

3. Work

Consider the challenges you face in the situation where you spend most of your daytime. What aspects of God's character does that situation most need and how can you demonstrate them?

4. Further debate

Watch *The West Wing* Season 2, Episode 3, "The Midterms" debate between President Bartlett and Dr Jacobs. (quoted in *Different Eyes*)

What point is being made and how do we understand the context of ethics in the Old Testament?

Resources

Further reading:

Thomas L. Trevethan, *The Beauty of God's Holiness* (IVP, 1995)

AW Tozer, *The Knowledge of the Holy* (HarperOne, 1978)

Richard Lovelace, *Dynamics of Spiritual Life* (IVP, 1979)

Music:

U2, "Yahweh", *How To Dismantle An Atomic Bomb* (Island, 2004)

Bible:

Exodus 3:1–14

Now Moses was tending the flock of Jethro his father-in-law, the priest of Midian, and he led the flock to the far side of the desert and came to Horeb, the mountain of God. There the angel of the LORD appeared to him in flames of fire from within a bush. Moses saw that though the bush was on fire it did not burn up. So Moses thought, "I will go over and see this strange sight—why the bush does not burn up."

When the LORD saw that he had gone over to look, God called to him from within the bush, "Moses! Moses!"

And Moses said, "Here I am."

"Do not come any closer," God said. "Take off your sandals, for the place where you are standing is holy ground." Then he said, "I am the God of your father, the God of Abraham, the God of Isaac and the God of Jacob." At this, Moses hid his face, because he was afraid to look at God.

The LORD said, "I have indeed seen the misery of my people in Egypt. I have heard them crying out because of their slave drivers, and I am concerned about their suffering. So I have come down to rescue them from the hand of the Egyptians and to bring them up out of that land into a good and spacious land, a land flowing with milk and honey—the home of the Canaanites, Hittites, Amorites, Perizzites, Hivites and Jebusites. And now the cry of the Israelites has reached me, and I have seen the way the Egyptians are oppressing them. So now, go. I am sending you to Pharaoh to bring my people the Israelites out of Egypt."

But Moses said to God, "Who am I, that I should go to Pharaoh and bring the Israelites out of Egypt?"

And God said, "I will be with you. And this will be the sign to you that it is I who have sent you: When you have brought the people out of Egypt, you will worship God on this mountain."

Moses said to God, "Suppose I go to the Israelites and say to them, 'The God of your fathers has sent me to you,' and they ask me, 'What is his name?' Then what shall I tell them?"

God said to Moses, "I AM WHO I AM. This is what you are to say to the Israelites: 'I AM has sent me to you.' "

Recommended Book

Steve Chalke and Alan Mann, *Different Eyes: The Art of Living Beautifully* (Zondervan)

The Example We Follow

Aim

To construct a framework for the development of ethical skills and habits based on the character of God.

Learning Objectives

To understand how Jesus lived beautifully.

To understand that learning to live well is, for us as for Jesus, based on developing the right instincts and habits.

Overview

We'll see in this session that:

- We tend to think that what we believe is correct. History shows that, like our ancestors, we need prophetic voices to keep us on track.

- Jesus is God's ultimate voice or word and keeps us on the straight and narrow.

- Jesus is the great storyteller, rather than a legislator. His stories nudge us to imagine and then participate in the beautiful life.

- Living beautifully is only possible when we walk in living relationship with Christ.

- Beautiful living emerges as we embrace daily discipline; because that's when we can respond rightly, instinctively to ethical dilemmas, large or small.

- Oppression and shame don't lead to life change. Beautiful living comes as we embrace vision. The knowledge that God loves us and believes in us is core to that vision.

- We are welcomed and included in the purposes of God so that we may cooperate with him in changing the world.

Jeff Lucas

SESSION 2

Why (theory)

"We make the mistake of thinking that biblical ethics are set in stone, when, in fact, they are set in a story – and the story makes all the difference."

In Session 1, Russell Rook said that the great question of the Bible is not "Does God exist?" but "What kind of God exists?" God calls us to participate in his unfolding story and his holiness, not to embrace a system of rules and ethics. God's law was given to the Exodus travellers as they journeyed, not before they set off. Their travelling was the reason for and the context of the revelation.

When we lose the plot, we end up with rules. Rules rely on a sense of duty and are to be obeyed regardless of the consequences, or consequentialism. The right choice is the one that produces more benefit than harm.

God's call to holiness involves character formation that results in us living beautifully, with our ethical decisions shaped by virtuous character. The revolutionary call of Jesus is the key to that life of development.

1. Walking in the way or mindlessly marching?

Jesus called his followers to walk with him as his apprentices, not invite him into their hearts. Isaiah says the core of true faith is: "This is the way, walk in it" (Isa 30:21). The early church was known as 'The Way' (Acts 9:2).

What began as walking can become marching to the drumbeat of religion, because we are prone to wander. So we need loud, sometimes shocking, voices from people unafraid to challenge the status quo. However, our natural response often is to dismiss them as heretics. Only later might we recognise that they were right, as one generation's heretic turns into the next generation's prophet.

"We need heretics to keep faith alive.... who will risk everything to challenge the prevailing religion of the day." (Cath Corlin, 'Hard-wired to belong', *The Online Journal*, The Royal Society of Arts, (Summer 2009) http://www.thersa. org/fellowship/journal/archive/summer-2009/features/hardwired-to-belong)

What areas of your life are controlled more by rules, or consequentialism, than your sense of participating in God's transforming story? When, why and how did that come about?

PAUSE FOR THOUGHT

What do we as the church typically do with dissenting voices? How can we allow voices on the edge to keep us on track without meandering into error?

At times in the past, revolutionary change and correction came about when bold women and men spoke up even though they were dismissed as heretics. People such as William Wilberforce, who confronted slavery, Martin Luther King, who led the African-American civil rights movement, and Beyers Naudé, who challenged his church's teaching on apartheid in South Africa.

History's greatest heretic – at least according to the religious barons of his day (Mark 2:7) – was Jesus.

In Session 1 we learned from Russell Rook that at the summit of world history God's holiness showed up in Jesus. Pure holiness joined with pure humanity and proved, once and for all, that the holy God is for us and with us. Jesus said he was the ultimate portrait of God (John 14:9).

> 'We must behold him [Jesus Christ] as the pivotal and cardinal reality, round which all life and history have moved.' (H.R. Mackintosh, *The Person of Jesus Christ* (T&T Clark, 2000) 50)

Jesus came to not only save us but also show us the way. He lived, died and lived again to give us life, and to show us how to live. He both taught the Sermon on the Mount and obviously lived it out.

The beautiful life is stunningly modelled in Jesus' self-control, prayerfulness, courage, compassion, generosity, risk-taking, gentleness, faith, wisdom and servanthood. His life is the ultimate example and his teaching, which carried amazing authority (Luke 4:32), makes great use of stories that provoke, challenge and comfort.

2. Story, character and an impossible mission

> "The telling of stories has a key part in educating us into the virtues." (Alasdair MacIntyre, *After Virtue: a study in moral theory* (Gerald Duckworth & Co Ltd, 1981) 214)

> "If you ask a Rabbi a question, you'll very likely get a story for an answer." (Michael E. Williams)

Jesus was not, as we have already said, a lawmaker. He was a storyteller. Stories stir the imagination, nudge us to change and grow, enable us to respond to ethical issues with good choices rather than a rulebook because our character has developed. We can choose well because we know we're part of God's 'big fat' story.

Talk of choices shouldn't be allowed to lead us to think that character change is about willpower and we make our ethical choices independently of God. Without his Spirit in us, Christian life is impossible.

> "This is impossible stuff." (G.K Chesterton, on the Sermon on the Mount)

> "Apart from me, you can do nothing." (John 15:5)

Jesus invites us to a life of surpassing righteousness, to a heart change that leads to right behaviour. But this is impossible unless he works in us. Martin Debelius says that the sermon reveals the will of God, however unreachable. While this is an overstatement, it is true that beautiful living is impossible outside of union with Christ.

Jesus' beautiful life was dependent on the Father, and John's Gospel especially tracks that dependent relationship. Jesus invites us to live in the same way – in dependency upon and cooperation with God.

Jesus shows us how to live, and then calls us to live exactly that way. He works in us, and we cooperate with him as he works.

Our hearts change as we partner with God in the process of life. A beautiful life is not the result of making crisis decisions in the face of a dilemma, but of training and discipline so we do the right thing naturally. The Orthodox fathers call this training "the beautiful fight". And Gregory of Nazianzus (330–390) once described it as being "an instrument that the Holy Spirit blows on and on which he plays." In *Mere Christianity* C.S. Lewis wrote that without Christ we are "tin soldiers".

> "Holiness is a habit, not a performance." (*Different Eyes*)

"The crying need for today is for people of faith to live faithfully." (Richard Foster, *The Challenge of the Disciplined Life: Christian Reflections on Money, Sex, and Power* (HarperOne, 1989). 1)

"The necessary materials for the building up of a saint are in every life. … it is not necessary to be hung on a cross in order to be crucified; an idle slander accepted meekly will do instead. It is not necessary to kiss a leper to secure self-discipline; a genuine effort to be kind … to a person we dislike intensely will do as well." (R. Somerset Ward)

3. Everyday and lifelong discipleship

'Ethics' suggests big picture choices, but the beautiful life includes choosing well in small decisions.

"If we only think of ethics as debating the big issues such as those to do with medicine, international justice, the environment, the economy, business, education and poverty, and dealing with moments of personal crisis, we make a huge mistake.

"It seems strange to say it, but ethics is about much more than all that. For all those who follow Christ, ethics is not about isolated actions, or big decisions, but about the whole process of becoming the sort of person God wills us to be and commits himself to making us.

"Ethics are essentially about everyday life – our passions and perceptions – and the slow cultivation of good habits and moral skills. All of which means that, in short, every moment, even the most mundane, is an opportunity for moral formation and development." (*Different Eyes*)

We are invited to walk every day with God and live every day beautifully. Doing this will inevitably impact our world.

PAUSE FOR THOUGHT

"I had a period of accelerated growth in the early years of faith, but confess to have settled down as the years go by."

Why is this true of so many Christians? What would you say to this person to encourage them to commit to continuous development?

"There have been meetings of only a moment which have left impressions for life, for eternity. No one can understand that mysterious thing we call influence ... [yet] every one of us continually exerts influence, either to heal, to bless, to leave marks of beauty; or to wound, to hurt, to poison, to stain other lives." (J.R. Miller, *The Building of Character* (AMG Publishers, 1975) 3)

We are called to be disciples in the small details of life, and to be lifelong followers. For Christ the process of growth and character development is continuous.

4. I have a dream: the Sermon on the Mount

"The Sermon on the Mount is a vision for what it means to be human and live beautifully." (*Different Eyes*)

"If we think of Jesus just sitting there, telling people how to behave, we miss what was really going on." (N.T. Wright, *The Challenge of Jesus* (SPCK, 2000))

The Sermon on the Mount has been terribly misunderstood. Far from adding to the intolerable burden that ordinary people felt as they floundered in a maze of Pharisaic legislation, Jesus brought words of liberation and hope. The Sermon on the Mount is not what historian John Seeley in 1866 in *Ecce Homo* called 'Christ's legislation'. It was his freedom charter and a call to imagine what life with God can be like. It was a call to ordinary people to change the world.

"The Beatitudes simply cannot be 'good news' if they are understood as a set of 'how-tos' for achieving blessedness. They would then only amount to a new legalism. They would impose a new brand of Pharisaism, a new way of closing the door." (Dallas Willard, *The Divine Conspiracy* (HarperSanFrancisco, 1998) 103)

"Don't bustle me. Don't now-then me." (Eeyore speaking in AA Milne, *The House at Pooh Corner* (Penguin Books Ltd, 1988) 164)

PAUSE FOR THOUGHT

Scan the Sermon on the Mount (Matt 5–7). How have we turned the good news into bad news?

People flocked to hear Jesus because he came with good news, not condemnation and shame. Albert Einstein once called him the luminous Nazarene. Many Christians live broken, shame-loaded lives.

5. Good news or bad?

> "Blessed are the sat upon, spat upon, ratted on." (Paul Simon, 'Blessed')

> "Touch me, take me to that other place. Teach me, I know I'm not a hopeless case." (U2, 'Beautiful Day')

The Sermon on the Mount is not only a call to beautiful living, but an incredible invitation to those who had been viewed as anything but beautiful – the ordinary people. Jesus told the followers of John the Baptist: "The poor are hearing the good news" (Matt 11:5 CEV).

Ordinary people are called to be world changers.

> "Typically people do not seek a faith. They encounter one through their ties to other people who already accept this faith. Doctrines take on flesh." (Rodney Stark, *The rise of Christianity: a sociologist reconsiders history* (Princeton University Press, 1996) 56))

The beautiful life is attractive and world changing. Ordinary people are called to be "the light of the world, the salt of the earth" (Matt 5:13-14). Jesus shows them that God believes in them.

6. Marching in step or jazz improvisation?

> "There are some who can read music and so are able to play the tune they see written down in front of them, and a jazz musician understands the structures and principles and roots behind the tune and so develops the ability to improvise with great skill in harmony with it." (*Different Eyes*)

"There's a lot more to music than notes on a page. It's about heart. It's about feelings, and moving people, and something beautiful and being alive and having fun." (Glen Holland in *Mr. Holland's Opus*, 1995)

Jazz musicians are able to improvise with great skill because they have totally immersed themselves in the technical principles of music. They can then bring their contribution in a spontaneous and free style because they are so well prepared.

Jesus goes beyond rules to the deeper meaning and heart/ life responses. The Pharisees had learned the tune, but Jesus plays jazz and he wants everyone to play jazz.

What

1. Vision and change

"Our developing character is a gift of God's Spirit – an act of his grace. But we are also asked to work to be part of his development." (Different Eyes)

"His divine power has given us everything we need for life and godliness through our knowledge of him who called us by his own glory and goodness. … For this very reason, make every effort to add to your faith goodness; and to goodness, knowledge; and to knowledge, self-control; and to self-control, perseverance; and to perseverance, godliness; and to godliness, brotherly kindness; and to brotherly kindness, love." (2 Peter 1:3-5)

"The vision which underlies spiritual transformation into Christ likeness, then, is a vision of life now and forever in God's will and presence. This is a vision that is given to humanity by God by revelation… it is not a vision that we could imagine on our own, though thinkers and artists have sometimes captured aspects of it." (Dallas Willard, *Renovation of the Heart: Putting on the Character of Christ* (NavPress, 2002) 87)

In *Renovation of the Heart,* Dallas Willard outlines three elements to change and growth – vision, intention and means, or VIM.

- We need a **vision** – of life as it could and should be lived with God

- We need **intention** – daily making good choices that are sustained by vision. Willard says, 'If the genuine intention is there, the deed invariably follows.'

- We need **means** – embrace study, meditation, prayer and sacrifice, learning from the 'saints' of history and other sources the ways in which character is formed and virtue becomes a way of life.

2. Examining where we are with prayer

"*Examen* comes from the Latin and refers to the tongue, or weight indicator, or a balance scale, hence conveying the idea of an accurate assessment of the true situation." (Richard Foster)

Foster distinguishes between two types of *examen*: examen of consciousness and examen of conscience.

In examen of consciousness we prayerfully reflect on our thoughts, feelings and actions to see how God has been at work among us and how we responded.

We might consider, for example, whether a neighbour's noise was more than a rude interruption during a quiet evening and just maybe was God urging us to be attentive to the pain and loneliness of those around us.

Perhaps in a glorious sunrise God was shouting about his love of beauty and inviting us to share it, but we were too sleepy or self-absorbed to notice.

In examen of conscience, on the other hand, we invite God to search the depths our heart. Far from being dreadful, it's a scrutiny of love.

We boldly recite the words of the psalmist: "Search me, O God, and know my heart; test me and know my thoughts. See if there is any wicked way in me and lead me in the way everlasting." (Psa 139:23–24)

Without apology or defence, for our own sakes, we ask God to see what is in us. It is for our good, our healing and our happiness.

The five steps are:

1. Recall you are in the presence of God.

2. Look over the events of the day with gratitude for the day's gifts.

3. Invite the Holy Spirit to help you evaluate your actions and attitudes with honesty and patience.

4. Review the day, making yourself aware of where Christ assisted your decisions and where you should have paused to receive his instructions.

5. A heart-to-heart talk with Jesus, sharing your thoughts on your actions, attitudes, feelings and interactions.

We say the Methodist Covenant Prayer (opposite) to soberly and thoughtfully recommit ourselves at this stage of our lives.

What could this mean practically in your own life?

PAUSE FOR THOUGHT

I am no longer my own but yours. Put me to what you will, rank me with whom you will; put me to doing, put me to suffering; let me be employed for you or laid aside for you, exalted for you or brought low for you; let me be full, let me be empty, let me have all things, let me have nothing; I freely and wholeheartedly yield all things to your pleasure and disposal.

And now, glorious and blessed God, Father, Son and Holy Spirit, you are mine and I am yours. So be it. And the covenant made on earth, let it be ratified in heaven.

Amen.

How

Choose one of these three scenarios. Now apply the VIM/examen tools and the Methodist Covenant to find a solution.

1. Business

You are a manager. Your company has the potential to expand, but there is a credit crunch. One advisor says you should cut back, another suggests striking out now for growth. What should you do? Apply the VIM tool.

2. Relational

You are a well-connected member of the community and church. Your daughter, who has a huge network of friends, has not got into her preferred secondary school. The only other school is failing, with issues of bullying, disruption and high staff turnover. You could move house, pretend your daughter lives at her grandmother's, send her to a private school you can't afford or do home-schooling. Apply the VIM tool.

3. Church

Your church calls an emergency meeting to discuss a financial crisis that has just been uncovered. There is a lot of anger that it wasn't uncovered earlier, especially as the church is raising money for a building project while a lot of members are struggling to make ends meet. You are chairing the meeting. First, use examen to determine where you are as you come to this meeting; second, use VIM to work out how to structure the meeting.

Resources

Further reading:

Dallas Willard, *Renovations of the Heart* (NAV Press, 2002)

N.T. Wright, *The Challenge of Jesus* (SPCK Publishing, 2000)

Dallas Willard, *The Divine Conspiracy* (Fount, 1998)

Gary Thomas, *The Beautiful Fight* (Zondervan, 2007)

Donald Kraybill, *The Upside Down Kingdom* (Herald, 2003)

Music:

Paul Simon, "Blessed", *Sounds of Silence* (Columbia, 1966)

U2, "Beautiful Day", *All That You Can't Leave Behind* (Island, 2000)

Miles Davis, *Kind of Blue* (Columbia Records, 1959)

Film:

Pay it Forward (Warner Brothers, 2000) directed by Mimi Leder

Bible:

Matthew 5:1–16

Now when he saw the crowds, he went up on a mountainside and sat down. His disciples came to him, and he began to teach them saying:

"Blessed are the poor in spirit,
        for theirs is the kingdom of heaven.
    Blessed are those who mourn,
        for they will be comforted.
    Blessed are the meek,
        for they will inherit the earth.
    Blessed are those who hunger and thirst for righteousness,
        for they will be filled.
    Blessed are the merciful,
        for they will be shown mercy.
    Blessed are the pure in heart,
        for they will see God.
    Blessed are the peacemakers,
        for they will be called sons of God.
    Blessed are those who are persecuted because of righteousness,
        for theirs is the kingdom of heaven.

"Blessed are you when people insult you, persecute you and falsely say all kinds of evil against you because of me. Rejoice and be glad, because great is your reward in heaven, for in the same way they persecuted the prophets who were before you.

"You are the salt of the earth. But if the salt loses its saltiness, how can it be made salty again? It is no longer good for anything, except to be thrown out and trampled by men.

"You are the light of the world. A city on a hill cannot be hidden. Neither do people light a lamp and put it under a bowl. Instead they put it on its stand, and it gives light to everyone in the house. In the same way, let your light shine before men, that they may see your good deeds and praise your Father in heaven."

Recommended Book

Stanley Hauerwas, Sam Wells and friends, *Living out Loud*, eds. Luke Bretherton and Russell Rook (Paternoster)

The Community We Belong To

Aim

To understand that the only way to develop a mature Christian ethic is within the context of community.

Learning Objectives

To know how a Christian ethical framework is distinct from other ethical approaches.

To recognise the hallmarks of the kind of community we need to belong to in order to live beautifully.

Overview

In this session we'll see that:

- We are all shaped by the stories of our lives. They shape the way we view life and determine how and what we decide throughout our lives.

- The way we 'do life' is not based on a universal agreement, but on the values of our communities. Therefore, our community is crucial to our formation as Christians.

- We are not isolated followers of Jesus. We do not learn how to make wise decisions and develop good habits on our own, but by being with other people.

- Jesus story will inspire us to live out his story as the story for all people, and will motivate us to throw ourselves into an honest, living and vibrant community.

Ruth Valerio

SESSION 3

Why (theory)

"We become who our story tells us we are." *(Different Eyes)*

In the first two sessions we looked at two foundations for the way we, as Christians, live:

Who God is: Yahweh, the God of holiness, revealed in the story of the people of Israel.

The example of Jesus: seen especially in the Sermon on the Mount.

Now, in this session, we turn our attention to the important role that community plays in shaping our ethics and helping us live our lives well.

Imagine your life story turned into a book or a film. What title would it have? Which episodes would make good drama or romantic comedy? Are there parts that felt like they belonged to a soap opera? What would be its theme, and how would you like it to finish? Sit with God and give him the space to talk with you through your thoughts on your life.

PAUSE FOR THOUGHT

1. The power of the story

Steven Spielberg's *The Prince of Egypt* depicts memorably the collision of two stories in Moses' life. Having been brought up as Pharaoh's son, the dominant story is of royalty, privilege and prestige. Moses lived accordingly. A chance encounter with his (unknown to him) sister began to suggest that there was another story of which he was unaware.

In the film, the stories collided when Moses saw hieroglyphics on a wall and discovered that his story was not only one of princedom but also linked inextricably to the Hebrew slaves. This realisation changed his life forever.

We are all shaped by our stories. For some of us those stories have been good. We grew up in a loving and stable family, school was a positive experience, we are successful in life and have done well for ourselves.

Others have stories of living under bad influences, of years spent fighting to break free from them. Most of our stories are probably a mixture of the good and the bad.

2. What is your wider story?

Of course, our stories are not just about our family background; they are also shaped by society, politics, media, community, education and popular culture.

> "For better or worse, we all have stories that shape who we are and how we respond. More than that, the communities in which we live, and even our society as a whole, has dominant narratives which exert huge influences in determining what we believe about ourselves, the world in which we live, and the way we should live in it." (*Different Eyes*)

In the previous session we looked at the Sermon on the Mount and saw the amazing picture of the beautiful life that Jesus lived; a life that was revolutionary and refreshing, liberating, challenging and world changing.

The stunning thing is that Jesus opened up his life and calls us to join with him in discovering how we can have beautiful lives too.

As his apprentices, our story is ultimately found in him. Nowhere is this expressed better than here: "If anyone is in Christ, he is a new creation; the old has gone, the new has come!" (1 Cor 5:17)

What incredible words.

Whatever our story is, it is picked up, redeemed, transformed, created anew in the story of Jesus. We no longer have to be shaped by the narrative of our life or the messages of our culture. We belong to Jesus and live accordingly.

3. The view from nowhere

The Jeremy Vine Show is a topical debate on Radio 2 that takes the biggest stories from the news and mixes in comments from 'experts' and feedback from the public. I find it excruciatingly frustrating because everyone has a different opinion and no one can reach agreement on anything!

In fact, *The Jeremy Vine Show* is the perfect example of what philosopher Alasdair MacIntyre in *After Virtue: A Theory of Justice* (Duckworth, 1985) calls the 'interminability' of modern debates on issues of morality.

What he means by this is that debates go on and on forever not just because no common agreement can be found, but because people have such different starting points.

Different starting points lead to different endings because there is no view from nowhere. We all have our own standpoint and particular perspective.

From the big ethical questions of the day down to the little attitudes, assumptions and decisions we take and make through the day, how we think and what we do is determined by the story in which we stand.

Take murder for example. There are cultures where a good son is expected to kill his parents at a certain age to ensure that they enter the afterlife physically active and energetic. Other cultures expect the community to look after their elderly people and hold them in the highest regard.

The key point is that there is no such thing as a universally agreed set of moral principles, as much as we might wish there were. We simply cannot get everyone to agree on any one particular thing.

> "What you see and hear depends a good deal on where you are standing; it also depends on what kind of a person you are." (C.S. Lewis, *The Magician's Nephew*)

4. The view from somewhere: Jesus Christ, Lord of all

Those of us who cherish our view as the only correct one may be feeling disorientated at this point, like the blind man in the introduction who was given sight.

We are the kind of people who are used to standing securely on our own viewpoint, which we have based firmly on Jesus and his Word, and the suggestion that it may actually be based on our own narratives and our way of seeing things could be scary.

If we acknowledge that there is no view from nowhere, how do we move forward? Where does a Christian ethic fit into all of this?

One possible route is to give in to the monster of relativism and say: "If it's okay for you it's okay for you, and if it's okay for me it's okay for me."

Relativism declares that we are all islands separated by vast oceans that can't be crossed. Your island is as valid as mine and I shouldn't try to get you onto my island, or vice versa. As Christians, we tuck ourselves up in our Christian morality but have no resources to impact the world around us.

"We are moving toward a dictatorship of relativism which does not recognise anything as for certain and which has as its highest goal one's own ego and one's own desires." (Pope Benedict XVI, Homily at eligendo Summo Pontifice Mass 18 April 2005)

Another possibility is to say that while there may be no universally agreed ethic, we can still affirm that there is an ethic for the universe. This is because we believe Jesus is Lord of the whole universe, and that his story, as revealed in the Bible and the Cross in particular, is true for all people.

"What if we dare to believe that this is God's universe, and he has revealed himself as he truly is through Jesus Christ? And what if, through that life, sacrificed on the cross, and by his subsequent resurrection, Jesus has defeated death and begun the work of the re-creation of all things? And what if one day this work will be completed as God finally wipes away every tear from every eye as his kingdom becomes fully-present? Daring to believe this will lead us to reach a very different conclusion about the moral framework in which we live, even though it may seem irrational to those who do not believe what we do." (Different Eyes)

We can have courage to live our lives as apprentices of Jesus, knowing that his story is the story for the whole world: a story of transformation and renewal. Along the way we invite others to join the story and take their parts in it.

PAUSE FOR THOUGHT

Has living in the story of Jesus ever led you to do something that didn't make sense to other people?

5. Tacit knowledge

How do we find our way in this age of uncertainty? How do we remain faithful to the Lord of the universe in a world where the harder we try to grasp absolutes the faster they slip away?

Consider two computer operators. The first types with two fingers, looking at the keyboard as they carefully poke each key. They can do it fairly quickly, but it's a thought-through process; each key has first to be deliberately found and then pressed. The second person touch-types. Their fingers dance over the keyboard automatically without them ever having to look at the keys.

The difference between these two is the difference between the way of living envisaged by the Enlightenment and the way of living that involves 'tacit knowledge'. Philosopher Michael Polanyi coined the phrase tacit knowledge in his book *Personal Knowledge: Towards a Post-Critical Philosophy* (Chicago University Press, 1974).

The Enlightenment led to a view of morality as something to be discovered by each individual on their own through a process of thought-through reflection.

Polanyi's tacit knowledge, however, is the result of learning a skill so thoroughly that it has become embedded – like riding a bike or swimming. A touch typist demonstrates muscle memory: an action has been repeated so often that it is 'natural' to do it without having to think explicitly how. There is no consciously thought-through action or decision.

And so, as Jeff Lucas showed us in the previous session, a follower of Jesus develops tacit knowledge by the virtues they practice every day, by living how Jesus lived. Our character is built up so that making a compassionate decision, taking a courageous step or thinking a wise thought is the natural thing to do.

"Enlightenment morality in Germany had spawned plenty of graduates who could get straight As in civil engineering, but it hadn't produced enough people who would refuse to use their skills to design the ovens of Dachau." (Brian McLaren, *Finding Our Way Again*, quoted in *Different Eyes*)

6. Me, a name I call myself

"Mark, you have hit upon one of my most serious concerns regarding 'self development'. You say you are not the person you would like to be. This begs many questions; why do you want to be like this 'other person', why is this 'other person' better, from where have you got your value judgements – if from other people, then by definition, you are not being yourself." (des troy commenting on Mark Boyle, http://www.justfortheloveofit.org/blog-1370-a-week-of-silence (accessed 20.10.2009))

Individualism has become one of the hallmarks of our era: we are independent, rational beings and our chief end is to realise our personal goals and desires with as little interference from outside as possible.

"I pattern my actions and life after what I want. No two people are alike. You might admire attributes in others, but use these only as a guide in improving yourself in your own unique way. I don't go for carbon copies. Individualism is sacred!" (Richard Chamberlain, interview 32, question 46, www.richard-chamberlain.co.uk)

The danger with the illustration of the two computer operators is that it gives the impression that a virtuous life can arise on its own. Compare them with a fantastic footballing partnership between two strikers. The goals they score don't happen by chance. They are the result of long practise together, with one person's skill developed through playing with the other.

Ethics is as much about *who we are* as *what we do*. We became who we are through the habits we developed. And we can develop our habits only through community, through interaction with other people. In community we learn 'tacit morality'. We learn habits and practices, both sinful and saintly, that become so ingrained they are our natural way of thinking and behaving.

> "Every local church should be a counter-cultural community working to break free of the tyranny of the detachment and individualism in which our society is soaked. Renewal comes, not from the wisdom and heroic actions of a few isolated 'super-thinkers', but rather through a community as it is shaped by the moral vision of the biblical story, as we seek to help each other live it out, day-by-day." *(Different Eyes)*

What

1. A Christ community

> "Now you are the body of Christ, and each one of you is a part of it." *(1 Cor 12:27)*

We are all members of a number of communities, but it is primarily the community of Christ that we belong to and that holds our allegiance. In his community we are part of a body and all play our own parts, yet we live and work together.

> "The reason for community is to help us follow Christ and to help us help others live Christlike lives." *(Andy Freeman and Pete Greig, Punk Monk: New Monasticism and the Ancient Art of Breathing (Regal Books, 2007))*

2. Communities of character

> "If it is true, then, that our habits and practices come through our rubbing shoulders with others, and if that impact can be both positive and negative, then the question we must ask ourselves is, 'What sort of community do I need to be a part of in order to live the kind of life that will reflect God's character – a life of faithfulness, forgiveness, generosity and wisdom?'" *(Different Eyes)*

The church provides a community in which to practise whole-life discipleship. That's all areas of life, not just the

PAUSE FOR THOUGHT

My husband and I have had other people living with us pretty much since the day we were married. We've had a whole variety of people come through our doors over the years: regular people from church, people outside of church,

overseas students, a pregnant lady, a guy who ended up in prison... all sorts! Although sometimes it'd be more comfortable just to live as a family with no one else, having others with us has challenged me in so many ways and whereas I always thought we had other people in to help change them, actually I've realised that it is me who has been changed in the process. I've learnt more about myself than I would've done through attending a hundred discipleship courses, and I think I have not just learnt but have changed too.

How have you developed most as a Christian and what practical implications does that have on the way we do church?

importance of work and the place of sex and alcohol. How we use money, how we talk about people, how we look after God's world, the way we parent, our doubts and many more things besides are open to challenge.

Think through the topics covered through the year in your church. Are they relevant? Are they practical? What things are missing?

We need to allow community members to share doubt and concern, worries and failures, and we need to do so ourselves. We need to ban tut-tutting and 'knowing looks' from the church community.

3. A community that calls us on an adventure

Jesus' apprentices wear rugged walking boots, not cosy slippers. There will be times when our decisions or actions make little sense to people outside the community.

Society is obsessed with making money, buying things and enhancing careers, and that puts so much focus on personal fulfilment that when our decisions don't follow that line we look strange. There is a difference between taking risks and being stupid, so we need to be in accountable relationships with wise people who help us discern between the two.

We should encourage one another to sometimes make decisions that are not on the safe side. And then be prepared to stand by and support them prayerfully and practically in those decisions. Bringing the church community together for regular periods of prayer and fasting will give God more room to speak, challenge and refresh.

> "If we listened to our intellect, we'd never have a love affair. We'd never have a friendship. We'd never go into business, because we'd be too cynical. Well, that's nonsense. You've got to jump off cliffs all the time and build your wings on the way down." (Ray Bradbury, quoted in *Business Wit and Wisdom* (Richard S. Zera, 2005))

PAUSE FOR THOUGHT

We are all part of various communities: at college or work, playing sports, in the club or pub, with or without Christians. Where are your communities? What do you get from each one and what do you give to them? What particular virtues or habits are needed in your different communities?

"The only person who never makes mistakes is the person who never does anything." (unknown)

"I am always doing that which I cannot do in order to learn how to do it." (Pablo Picasso)

4. A community where we don't fear to be confronted or face conflict

How will we ever grow in our understanding of ourself if we never let anyone tell us our weaknesses? These things should not be spoken harshly or inappropriately, but with truth and grace. We won't grow as community until we learn how to deal with conflict.

Guidelines for conflict resolution:
(contributed by 3D Coaching Ltd.)

1. **Listen** carefully without worrying about sorting the issue. It is a great diffuser if you listen to someone and then demonstrate that you have listened.

2. **Reflect back** what you have heard – don't be judgmental, use their words – "I heard you say you feel I am rude" "You don't like how I approach you…."

3. **Check** you have heard everything and that you have understood it in the way they meant you to. Eg: "I heard you say a, b, c – Is that correct? Have I missed anything?"

4. **Seek to be understood:** "Can I now tell you how I feel?" Use I statements. Eg: "I feel you are being aggressive towards me when you say…" "I feel angry when you talk to others and not to me."

5. If you can, **give a clear, brief example:** Remember no one can change what has already happened. Hindsight is a wonderful thing – use it to learn and move forward more positively.

6. Once both of you have said how you feel you need to **co-design** the solution for the future. Eg: "OK, knowing

how we both feel – how can we take this forward?" It is really important that as you co-design you are both **honest** about what works for you and what doesn't. "I hear what you say and I am uncomfortable about us agreeing never to talk in the office ... what can we do instead? Is it good for us both?" Use past experiences not to blame but to learn from and to positively inform the future.

7. Sum up the co-designed solutions: "**I think we agreed to:** a,b,c." It is most powerful if these are agreed and written down at the time.

8. **Check** "Is that correct? Is there anything else?"

9. And then the really powerful question : "**How are we going to be kind in dealing with each other if we get it wrong (or if we continue to have different opinions)?**"

"We are called to accept with compassion and humility the particular fragility, complexity, and incompleteness of each brother. Our diversity and our brokenness mean that tensions and friction are inevitably woven into the fabric of everyday life. They are not to be regarded as signs of failure. Christ uses them for our conversion as we grow in mutual forbearance and learn to let go of the pride that drives us to control and reform our brothers on our own terms." (The Society of St John the Evangelist, *Living In Hope: A rule of life for today* (Canterbury Press, 1997) p11)

"Peace is not the absence of conflict but the presence of creative alternatives for responding to conflict – alternatives to passive or aggressive responses, alternatives to violence." (Dorothy Thompson)

"Truth springs from argument among friends." (David Hume)

"There are three ways of dealing with difference: domination, compromise, and integration. By domination only one side gets what it wants; by compromise neither side gets what it wants; by integration we find a way by which both sides may get what they wish." (Mary Parker Follett)

"We are not going to deal with the violence in our communities, our homes, and our nation, until we learn to deal with the basic ethic of how we resolve our disputes and to place an emphasis on peace in the way we relate to one another." (Marian Wright Edelman)

5. A community where we can find, and be, moral mentors

"We learn good habits by watching people with good habits." (Different Eyes)

Are there older, wiser people around you who you would like to learn from? Ask them if you could spend some time with them. Be creative in how you do that. Are there people you could invest some of your wisdom and experience into? Invite them out for a cup of coffee or have them round for a meal. Find ways of making yourself available to others.

"There can be no vulnerability without risk; there can be no community without vulnerability; there can be no peace, and ultimately no life, without community." (M. Scott Peck)

"Wounds from a friend can be trusted, but an enemy multiplies kisses." (Prov 27:6)

"Mentor: someone whose hindsight can become your foresight." (Anon)

How

Apply the guidelines for conflict resolution to one of these scenarios.

1. Work

You are on a team that is falling behind schedule on a project. There has been a lack of focus from the start, and some team members are now refusing to cooperate because of blame-throwing. You are particularly upset. Your closest friend at work seems to be the key trouble-maker and your job is at risk if the project fails.

2. Relational

You haven't spoken to your sister since a legal brawl over inheritance eight years ago. You recently became a Christian and want to take steps to restore the relationship. Put together an action plan with practical ideas to prevent old wounds from causing further pain.

3. Church

You are a long-standing and active church member. You disagree with the church leadership's new stance on divorce and remarriage. How do you go about finding a way to agree/disagree?

4. Further debate

To what extent is it possible to be a churchless Christian?

Resources

Further reading:

Stefan Smart, *Deeper: Contemplative Prayer for Charismatic Christians* (New Wine Press, 2008)

Joshua Harris, *Stop Dating the Church: Fall in Love with the Family of God* (Multnomah Press, 2009)

Film:

Looking for Eric (2009) directed by Ken Loach

Bible:

Hebrews 10:16–25

"This is the covenant I will make with them after that time, says the Lord. I will put my laws in their hearts, and I will write them on their minds."

Then he adds:

"Their sins and lawless acts I will remember no more."

And where these have been forgiven, there is no longer any sacrifice for sin.

Therefore, brothers, since we have confidence to enter the Most Holy Place by the blood of Jesus, by a new and living way opened for us through the curtain, that is, his body, and since we have a great priest over the house of God, let us draw near to God with a sincere heart in full assurance of faith, having our hearts sprinkled to cleanse us from a guilty conscience and having our bodies washed with pure water. Let us hold unswervingly to the hope we profess, for he who promised is faithful. And let us consider how we may spur one another on toward love and good deeds. Let us not give up meeting together, as some are in the habit of doing, but let us encourage one another—and all the more as you see the Day approaching.

Recommended Book

Krish Kandiah,
Just Politics
(Authentic)

The World We Want To See

Aim

To learn how we journey towards the future we want to see.

Learning Objectives

To enable us to engage in the public realm.

To understand the ongoing developmental nature of Christian ethics.

Overview

In the session we'll see that:

The options for engagement in the world require us to ask:

- How do we position ourselves in relation to the political and social structures?

- How do we put our faith into action?

The answers have a huge impact on the way we do church and how we do ethics.

And we'll ask:

- What's right and wrong about right and wrong?

- In the end, what's the end of our ethics?

Pete
Broadbent

SESSION 4

Why (theory)

Superkidz Trust is based on one of the most deprived housing estates in London. Superkidz runs community outreach to support families, and children's sessions, which give children and young people a safe, inspiring place to play and develop. Nick Russell, whose wife Helen started the initiative, says: "God loves them more than they could imagine; we're helping them to understand that."

When churches engage with their communities in this way, they're doing the ethics of Jesus.

True church – the community of the baptised – lives the life of the eucharist. And in the communion service, however we celebrate it and whatever we call it, we're sent out with eyes wide open to livemissionally – sent just as Jesus was sent (John 20:21) – and sent to live eucharistically – thankful for the gifts of God in creation and wanting to share his gifts and love with the world.

1. Take a satnav check – where are we?

I've got a mate who's navigationally challenged. He has no map, either in his head or on paper. He can find his way to places only once he's entered the postcode in his satnav – and he couldn't tell you how he got somewhere, only that he'd arrived once his satnav told him so.

Something has happened in contemporary culture that means the Christian church has begun to lose its map of where we are in relation to society. But there's no postcode, no agreed satnav to help us position ourselves and work out how to engage in the public sphere.

Many Christians would say that we are now living in Post-Christendom:

How is my church doing the ethics of Jesus?

"You may not have noticed or cared, since it has
had so little effect recently, but that dubiously vain
rooster called Christendom – the organisational
inbreeding of religion, culture and state – has
gone the way of all flesh. … Make no mistake: the
cultural phenomenon of Christendom is dead."

(James D Berkley, *Essential Christianity* (Zondervan, 2001) 10)

2. How might we adapt to this fast-changing context?

Radical exponents of post-Christendom theory believe
Christians now have a chance to reinvent the way in which
we 'do' the faith, and that we're better off without a state
church, establishment and the pretence of being a Christian
country. The question they pose is: "How do we live
authentically in Babylon?"

"As Christians enter the twenty-first century,
they do so as exiles, strangers and pilgrims,
aliens in a strange land. They will need to learn
the strategies of survival and to sing the songs
of Zion in the midst of Babylon." (Kenneth Leech
http://www.anglocatholicsocialism.org/jubileepeople.html,
quoted in *Different Eyes*)

Others assert that we're still at heart **a Christian country**.
They point to the fact that UK laws, institutions, art and
literature have been shaped by the Christian story, and argue
that we need to continue to affirm and assert that Christian
identity. Christendom, according to this viewpoint, is
valuable and to be treasured and nurtured.

A third view holds that **we live at the cusp of Christendom
and secularism** and that a transition from one to the
other may be in progress, but that we live in parallel and
overlapping expressions of the two. There are areas of life
where Christendom still has meaning, and others where a
secular consensus is emerging. This makes the task of the
Christian church more complex.

Two contrasting models are often used of the way in which Christians relate to their culture:

- **Resident aliens** (Stanley Hauerwas, Gilbert T. Rowe professor of theological ethics at Duke University Divinity School)

- **Critical solidarity** (a phrase often used of itself by the Church of England)

Those who see the church as being 'in exile' criticise the Christendom approach as having been assimilated by those in power; those who speak of 'critical solidarity' believe the church should not surrender its place in society but seek to use it for the common good, working with and alongside the structures of the state.

Underpinning both approaches is the idea that the church is called to be distinctive and bear distinctive witness to its counter-cultural values, living the life of Jesus as a challenge to the world.

"[The distinctive church seeks to] influence the world by being the church, that is, by being something the world is not and can never be, lacking the gift of faith and vision, which is ours in Christ. The confessing church seeks to be the visible church, a place, clearly visible to the world, in which people are faithful to their promises, love their enemies, tell the truth, honour the poor, suffer for righteousness and thereby testify to the amazing community-creating power of God." (Stanley Hauerwas and William H. Willimon, *Resident Aliens: Life in the Christian Colony* (Abingdon Press, 1993) p.46)

"The church exists ... to set up in the world a new sign which is radically dissimilar to [the world's] own manner and which contradicts it in a way which is full of promise." (Karl Barth, *Church Dogmatics*, quoted in Stanley Hauerwas and William H. Willimon, *Resident Aliens: Life in the Christian Colony* (Abingdon Press, 1993) 83)

PAUSE FOR THOUGHT

Which of these models (resident aliens or critical solidarity) of how the church operates rings most true in your local church experience? What insights can we gain from each of these models?

3. How can the church bear more distinctive witness to Christ?

A major challenge to the distinctive church is how to express its distinctiveness. Some would argue that our ethics are best expressed by living them out.

> "The church doesn't have a social strategy; the church is a social strategy. Our story is our morality! Churches are communities that create countercultural people – shaped by, and living out, a different story. Our task is to tell the story; to live in the story; to live the ethic; to be the ethic." *(Different Eyes)*

Others would point to the importance of the church's historic role in shaping and forming legislation and lobbying government, thus achieving important changes in the way in which laws are enacted.

Of course, as with so much, it's a question of both-and. For example, on the question of abortion, Christians have throughout the ages been at the forefront of agencies caring for those with unwanted pregnancies as well as being involved in the public debate about length of term, the rights of women and the sanctity of life.

Where the church's witness has been less than useful is where it has campaigned stridently and been heard only as being anti-abortion or pro-life – mere slogans.

> "No clever language or arguments can substitute for the necessity of the church to be a community of people who embody our language about God. Our churches are our theology. Any and every Christian ethical position is only made credible by the action of the church." *(Different Eyes)*

PAUSE FOR THOUGHT

How is your local church perceived – as bad news, good news, or no news?

What would our churches look like if they became communities where we worked at ethical questions together, doing our thinking in the context of the questions raised for us by our local communities?

4. What's right and wrong about right and wrong?

The popularity of WWJD – What Would Jesus Do? – bracelets points up a big question about how we do ethics. Although a helpful litmus test that has captured the imagination of many young people, it's impossible to answer WWJD in relation to most of the big questions.

This is partly because the Gospels tell us a limited amount of the story of Jesus, and partly because Jesus never faced the moral and ethical questions we face today.

Jesus hasn't invited us to ask him what he would do, he has invited us to journey with him as individuals and community. We can't just sign up to a set of rules. Making ethical decisions is about cultivating a relationship with Jesus and working at following him together.

> "Authentic Christianity is not learning a set of doctrines.... It is a walk, a supernatural walk with a living, dynamic, communicating God. Thus the heart and soul of the Christian life is learning to hear God's voice and developing the courage to do what he tells us to do." (Bill Hybels, *Too Busy Not to Pray: slowing down to be with God* (Intervarsity Press, 1998) 125)

> "It is wise to remember that even our best thinking and behaviour is never fully, finally Christian, but only ever more or less Christian than it was previously. Whenever we forget this, instead of Christ judging our ideas, his name ends up being used to justify our behaviours – including, unfortunately, both our ancient and modern crusades." (*Different Eyes*)

What might the future described here look like? Overleaf is an attempt to imagine what the future might look like for a community based on Revelation 21. Write your own version for your own church or community.

PAUSE FOR THOUGHT

5. In the end, what's the end of our ethics?

Some approaches to ethics concentrate on outcomes – what's the end in view when we make our decisions? Christians have a bigger end in view – the kingdom of God and the future of a new heaven and a new earth. The Greek word *telos* means 'end' or 'completion' and it is to the end that we need to look as we live for Jesus Christ.

Ethicist Alasdair MacIntyre suggests that we should think of our lives as a story, a narrative unity, governed by a telos. He says that no ethical system is intelligible or motivational if it isn't 'teleological', meaning it must include an account of the telos, purpose or meaning of life.

"Empowered by God's Spirit, we are active moral agents in the world, as we work to bring in the kingdom of God on earth as it is in heaven. Or, to put it theologically, our ethics, our values, should all be eschatological choices." *(Different Eyes)*

So here's the challenge. To live and see with different eyes, and to walk into God's future with our eyes wide open.

What

Revelation 21

It was 8 o'clock on Monday morning.
I was standing by Lambeth North station.
And I saw a new London coming down from the heavens.
I saw a teenager leaping out of bed with joy,
laughing with the freshness of the morning.
I saw elderly ladies skipping down Kennington Road
I saw children paddling in the River Thames.
I saw a football match in Kennington Park and the
teams were mixed people from every people group:
asylum seekers and taxi drivers, policemen and
prisoners, pensioners and politicians. People from
every race and class playing and laughing in the sun.
I saw a street party where the people were eating
and dancing because there was hope again.

And I looked across the community of South
London; a community of hope, a community
of grace, a community of warmth.
And, in the clearness of the morning, I looked
down into the Elephant & Castle and there was
no more asthma, no more unwanted pregnancies,
no more debt, no more violence, no more
overcrowding and nobody was too busy.

Chalke and Mann, *Different Eyes*, 157, 'Revelation 21' was adapted with
permission by Dave Steell/Steve Chalke from 'The New Glasgow' by Doug
Gay in Baker and Gay, *Alternative Worship* (SPCK 2003).

The River Thames was flowing with crystal-clear water.
There were no more needles and condoms in the park.
No more sorrow of family breakdown.
No more poverty.
No more need.
No more unemployment or mind-numbing jobs.
No more hopelessness.
No more sadness and tears, only joy and laughter.
No more discrimination.
No more drunken clubbing. No threats, no fears.

The dividing walls were gone.
Families and neighbours were restored.
There was no more rubbish, no dealers, no
guns, no knives, no dangerous dogs
There were no racial tensions, just one
harmonious mix in technicolour.

And I looked and I saw kids playing football in the
streets, and neighbours cheering them on.
I saw homes without locks on the doors, where
a welcome was always guaranteed.
I saw a playground with climbing frames that
weren't rusty, where children threw themselves in
the air without fear of harm, where the teenagers
helped the little ones up to the highest climbs.

I saw a London where neighbours shared favours,
and returned them without pressure or obligation.
I saw a London where hearts were unbroken,
partnerships are lasting, peaceful and happy.
I saw a London where families eat and play together.
I saw a London where tears were wiped away.

Square mile

Think about your community in terms of the square mile around your church/home. Reaching out to that community should involve a four-fold approach that reflects the biblical mandate for mission and has the initials MILE. (see www.eauk. org/squaremile)

Mercy – demonstrating God's compassion for the poor. Consider the practical needs in your square mile. What are church members already doing to meet these needs? What more could be done at an individual or church level?

Influence – being salt and light in the public life of the community. What are the main community influences in your area (radio, schools, hospitals, councils)? How are Christians represented in those areas? What more could be done at an individual or church level?

Life Discipleship – equipping Christians for missional living as workers and neighbours. What does it mean to be a Christian at work, at the school gate, in the doctor's waiting room? How can you make disciples who can make disciples?

Evangelism – faithful and relevant communication of the gospel. How can we best explain the gospel to the people in our square mile? If someone wanted to find out about the Christian faith, how would they go about it? What special events or courses could be run to help them?

How

Choose one scenario and apply the square mile principles.

1. Work

Write out Revelation 21 with your work environment in mind. How does knowing the *telos* for your workspace help motivate you for living distinctively at work?

2. Church

Your church is well-known for its mid-week youth activities, but on Sunday most people are over 50. How can you use the square mile approach to work out what church members are involved in, and how they can build on that to draw people to faith?

3. Relational

Audit your personal or family diary. How do you invest the time outside of work and church events? What difference would a personal square mile approach make to your kingdom time investment?

Resources

Book:

Tom Wright, *Surprised by Hope* (SPCK Publishing, 2007)

Film:

Knowing (2009) directed by Alex Proyas, rated 15

Television:

Flashforward (2009) Channel Five

Bible:

Romans 13:1–7

[1]Everyone must submit himself to the governing authorities, for there is no authority except that which God has established. The authorities that exist have been established by God. [2]Consequently, he who rebels against the authority is rebelling against what God has instituted, and those who do so will bring judgment on themselves. [3]For rulers hold no terror for those who do right, but for those who do wrong. Do you want to be free from fear of the one in authority? Then do what is right and he will commend you. [4]For he is God's servant to do you good. But if you do wrong, be afraid, for he does not bear the sword for nothing. He is God's servant, an agent of wrath to bring punishment on the wrongdoer. [5]Therefore, it is necessary to submit to the authorities, not only because of possible punishment but also because of conscience.

[6]This is also why you pay taxes, for the authorities are God's servants, who give their full time to governing. [7]Give everyone what you owe him: If you owe taxes, pay taxes; if revenue, then revenue; if respect, then respect; if honour, then honour.

Revelation 13:1–18

[1]And the dragon stood on the shore of the sea.

And I saw a beast coming out of the sea. He had ten horns and seven heads, with ten crowns on his horns, and on each head a blasphemous name. [2]The beast I saw resembled a leopard, but had feet like those of a bear and a mouth like that of a lion. The dragon gave the beast his power and his throne and great authority. [3]One of the heads of the beast seemed to have had a fatal wound, but the fatal wound had been healed. The whole world was astonished and followed the beast. [4]Men worshipped the dragon because he had given authority to the beast, and they also worshipped the beast and asked, Who is like the beast? Who can make war against him?

[5]The beast was given a mouth to utter proud words and blasphemies and to exercise his authority for forty-two months. [6]He opened his mouth to blaspheme God, and to slander his name and his dwelling-place and those who live in heaven. [7]He was given power to make war against the saints and to conquer them. And he was given authority over every tribe, people, language and nation. [8]All inhabitants of the earth will worship the beast—all whose names have not been written in the book of life belonging to the Lamb that was slain from the creation of the world.

[9]He who has an ear, let him hear.

[10]If anyone is to go into captivity, into captivity he will go.
If anyone is to be killed with the sword, with the sword he will be killed.

This calls for patient endurance and faithfulness on the part of the saints.

[11]Then I saw another beast, coming out of the earth. He had two horns like a lamb, but he spoke like a dragon. [12]He exercised all the authority of the first beast on his behalf, and made the earth and its inhabitants worship the first beast, whose fatal wound had been healed. [13]And he performed great and miraculous signs, even causing fire to come down

from heaven to earth in full view of men. [14]Because of the signs he was given power to do on behalf of the first beast, he deceived the inhabitants of the earth. He ordered them to set up an image in honour of the beast who was wounded by the sword and yet lived. [15]He was given power to give breath to the image of the first beast, so that it could speak and cause all who refused to worship the image to be killed. [16]He also forced everyone, small and great, rich and poor, free and slave, to receive a mark on his right hand or on his forehead, [17]so that no-one could buy or sell unless he had the mark, which is the name of the beast or the number of his name.

[18]This calls for wisdom. If anyone has insight, let him calculate the number of the beast, for it is man's number. His number is 666.

Revelation 21

[1]Then I saw a new heaven and a new earth, for the first heaven and the first earth had passed away, and there was no longer any sea. [2]I saw the Holy City, the new Jerusalem, coming down out of heaven from God, prepared as a bride beautifully dressed for her husband. [3]And I heard a loud voice from the throne saying, "Now the dwelling of God is with men, and he will live with them. They will be his people, and God himself will be with them and be their God. [4]He will wipe every tear from their eyes. There will be no more death or mourning or crying or pain, for the old order of things has passed away."

[5]He who was seated on the throne said, "I am making everything new!" Then he said, "Write this down, for these words are trustworthy and true."

[6]He said to me: "It is done. I am the Alpha and the Omega, the Beginning and the End. To him who is thirsty I will give to drink without cost from the spring of the water of life. [7]He who overcomes will inherit all this, and I will be his God and he will be my son. [8]But the cowardly, the unbelieving, the vile, the murderers, the sexually immoral, those who practise magic arts, the idolaters and all liars—their place will be in the fiery lake of burning sulphur. This is the second death."

⁹One of the seven angels who had the seven bowls full of the seven last plagues came and said to me, "Come, I will show you the bride, the wife of the Lamb." ¹⁰And he carried me away in the Spirit to a mountain great and high, and showed me the Holy City, Jerusalem, coming down out of heaven from God. ¹¹It shone with the glory of God, and its brilliance was like that of a very precious jewel, like a jasper, clear as crystal. ¹²It had a great, high wall with twelve gates, and with twelve angels at the gates. On the gates were written the names of the twelve tribes of Israel. ¹³There were three gates on the east, three on the north, three on the south and three on the west. ¹⁴The wall of the city had twelve foundations, and on them were the names of the twelve apostles of the Lamb.

¹⁵The angel who talked with me had a measuring rod of gold to measure the city, its gates and its walls. ¹⁶The city was laid out like a square, as long as it was wide. He measured the city with the rod and found it to be 12,000 stadia in length, and as wide and high as it is long. ¹⁷He measured its wall and it was 144 cubits thick, by man's measurement, which the angel was using. ¹⁸The wall was made of jasper, and the city of pure gold, as pure as glass. ¹⁹The foundations of the city walls were decorated with every kind of precious stone. The first foundation was jasper, the second sapphire, the third chalcedony, the fourth emerald, ²⁰the fifth sardonyx, the sixth carnelian, the seventh chrysolite, the eighth beryl, the ninth topaz, the tenth chrysoprase, the eleventh jacinth, and the twelfth amethyst. ²¹The twelve gates were twelve pearls, each gate made of a single pearl. The great street of the city was of pure gold, like transparent glass.

²²I did not see a temple in the city, because the Lord God Almighty and the Lamb are its temple. ²³The city does not need the sun or the moon to shine on it, for the glory of God gives it light, and the Lamb is its lamp. ²⁴The nations will walk by its light, and the kings of the earth will bring their splendour into it. ²⁵On no day will its gates ever be shut, for there will be no night there. ²⁶The glory and honour of the nations will be brought into it. ²⁷Nothing impure will ever enter it, nor will anyone who does what is shameful or deceitful, but only those whose names are written in the Lamb's book of life.

Recommended DVD

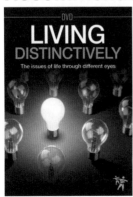

*Living
Distinctively,*
Elevation